Visitors

Who's visiting:

Today's Date:

How we spent our time together:

When I will come again:

Visitors

Who's visiting:

Today's Date:

How we spent our time together:

When I will come again:

Visitors

Who's visiting:

Today's Date:

How we spent our time together:

When I will come again:

Visitors

Who's visiting:

Today's Date:

How we spent our time together:

When I will come again:

Visitors

Who's visiting:

Today's Date:

How we spent our time together:

When I will come again:

Visitors

Who's visiting:

Today's Date:

How we spent our time together:

When I will come again:

Visitors

Who's visiting:

Today's Date:

How we spent our time together:

When I will come again:

Visitors

Who's visiting:

Today's Date:

How we spent our time together:

When I will come again:

Visitors

Who's visiting:

Today's Date:

How we spent our time together:

When I will come again:

Visitors

Who's visiting:

Today's Date:

How we spent our time together:

When I will come again:

Visitors

Who's visiting:

Today's Date:

How we spent our time together:

When I will come again:

Visitors

Who's visiting:

Today's Date:

How we spent our time together:

When I will come again:

Visitors

Who's visiting:

Today's Date:

How we spent our time together:

When I will come again:

Visitors

Who's visiting:

Today's Date:

How we spent our time together:

When I will come again:

Visitors

Who's visiting:

Today's Date:

How we spent our time together:

When I will come again:

Visitors

Who's visiting:

Today's Date:

How we spent our time together:

When I will come again:

Visitors

Who's visiting:

Today's Date:

How we spent our time together:

When I will come again:

Visitors

Who's visiting:

Today's Date:

How we spent our time together:

When I will come again:

Visitors

Who's visiting:

Today's Date:

How we spent our time together:

When I will come again:

Visitors

Who's visiting:

Today's Date:

How we spent our time together:

When I will come again:

Visitors

Who's visiting:

Today's Date:

How we spent our time together:

When I will come again:

Visitors

Who's visiting:

Today's Date:

How we spent our time together:

When I will come again:

Visitors

Who's visiting:

Today's Date:

How we spent our time together:

When I will come again:

Visitors

Who's visiting:

Today's Date:

How we spent our time together:

When I will come again:

Visitors

Who's visiting:

Today's Date:

How we spent our time together:

When I will come again:

Visitors

Who's visiting:

Today's Date:

How we spent our time together:

When I will come again:

Visitors

Who's visiting:

Today's Date:

How we spent our time together:

When I will come again:

Visitors

Who's visiting:

Today's Date:

How we spent our time together:

When I will come again:

Visitors

Who's visiting:

Today's Date:

How we spent our time together:

When I will come again:

Visitors

Who's visiting:

Today's Date:

How we spent our time together:

When I will come again:

Visitors

Who's visiting:

Today's Date:

How we spent our time together:

When I will come again:

Visitors

Who's visiting:

Today's Date:

How we spent our time together:

When I will come again:

Visitors

Who's visiting:

Today's Date:

How we spent our time together:

When I will come again:

Visitors

Who's visiting:

Today's Date:

How we spent our time together:

When I will come again:

Visitors

Who's visiting:

Today's Date:

How we spent our time together:

When I will come again:

Visitors

Who's visiting:

Today's Date:

How we spent our time together:

When I will come again:

Visitors

Who's visiting:

Today's Date:

How we spent our time together:

When I will come again:

Visitors

Who's visiting:

Today's Date:

How we spent our time together:

When I will come again:

Visitors

Who's visiting:

Today's Date:

How we spent our time together:

When I will come again:

Visitors

Who's visiting:

Today's Date:

How we spent our time together:

When I will come again:

Visitors

Who's visiting:

Today's Date:

How we spent our time together:

When I will come again:

Visitors

Who's visiting:

Today's Date:

How we spent our time together:

When I will come again:

Visitors

Who's visiting:

Today's Date:

How we spent our time together:

When I will come again:

Visitors

Who's visiting:

Today's Date:

How we spent our time together:

When I will come again:

Visitors

Who's visiting:

Today's Date:

How we spent our time together:

When I will come again:

Visitors

Who's visiting:

Today's Date:

How we spent our time together:

When I will come again:

Visitors

Who's visiting:

Today's Date:

How we spent our time together:

When I will come again:

Visitors

Who's visiting:

Today's Date:

How we spent our time together:

When I will come again:

Visitors

Who's visiting:

Today's Date:

How we spent our time together:

When I will come again:

Visitors

Who's visiting:

Today's Date:

How we spent our time together:

When I will come again:

Visitors

Who's visiting:

Today's Date:

How we spent our time together:

When I will come again:

Visitors

Who's visiting:

Today's Date:

How we spent our time together:

When I will come again:

Visitors

Who's visiting:

Today's Date:

How we spent our time together:

When I will come again:

Visitors

Who's visiting:

Today's Date:

How we spent our time together:

When I will come again:

Visitors

Who's visiting:

Today's Date:

How we spent our time together:

When I will come again:

Visitors

Who's visiting:

Today's Date:

How we spent our time together:

When I will come again:

Visitors

Who's visiting:

Today's Date:

How we spent our time together:

When I will come again:

Visitors

Who's visiting:

Today's Date:

How we spent our time together:

When I will come again:

Visitors

Who's visiting:

Today's Date:

When I will come again:

How we spent our time together:

Visitors

Who's visiting:

Today's Date:

How we spent our time together:

When I will come again:

Visitors

Who's visiting:

Today's Date:

How we spent our time together:

When I will come again:

Visitors

Who's visiting:

Today's Date:

How we spent our time together:

When I will come again:

Visitors

Who's visiting:

Today's Date:

How we spent our time together:

When I will come again:

Visitors

Who's visiting:

Today's Date:

How we spent our time together:

When I will come again:

Visitors

Who's visiting:

Today's Date:

How we spent our time together:

When I will come again:

Visitors

Who's visiting:

Today's Date:

How we spent our time together:

When I will come again:

Visitors

Who's visiting:

Today's Date:

How we spent our time together:

When I will come again:

Visitors

Who's visiting:

Today's Date:

How we spent our time together:

When I will come again:

Visitors

Who's visiting:

Today's Date:

How we spent our time together:

When I will come again:

Visitors

Who's visiting:

Today's Date:

How we spent our time together:

When I will come again:

Visitors

Who's visiting:

Today's Date:

How we spent our time together:

When I will come again:

Visitors

Who's visiting:

Today's Date:

How we spent our time together:

When I will come again:

Visitors

Who's visiting:

Today's Date:

How we spent our time together:

When I will come again:

Visitors

Who's visiting:

Today's Date:

How we spent our time together:

When I will come again:

Visitors

Who's visiting:

Today's Date:

How we spent our time together:

When I will come again:

Visitors

Who's visiting:

Today's Date:

How we spent our time together:

When I will come again:

Visitors

Who's visiting:

Today's Date:

How we spent our time together:

When I will come again:

Visitors

Who's visiting:

How we spent our time together:

Today's Date:

When I will come again:

Visitors

Who's visiting:

Today's Date:

How we spent our time together:

When I will come again:

Visitors

Who's visiting:

Today's Date:

How we spent our time together:

When I will come again:

Visitors

Who's visiting:

Today's Date:

How we spent our time together:

When I will come again:

Visitors

Who's visiting:

Today's Date:

How we spent our time together:

When I will come again:

Visitors

Who's visiting:

Today's Date:

How we spent our time together:

When I will come again:

Visitors

Who's visiting:

Today's Date:

How we spent our time together:

When I will come again:

Visitors

Who's visiting:

Today's Date:

How we spent our time together:

When I will come again:

Visitors

Who's visiting:

Today's Date:

How we spent our time together:

When I will come again:

Visitors

Who's visiting:

Today's Date:

How we spent our time together:

When I will come again:

Visitors

Who's visiting:

Today's Date:

How we spent our time together:

When I will come again:

Visitors

Who's visiting:

Today's Date:

How we spent our time together:

When I will come again:

Visitors

Who's visiting:

Today's Date:

How we spent our time together:

When I will come again:

Visitors

Who's visiting:

Today's Date:

How we spent our time together:

When I will come again:

Visitors

Who's visiting:

Today's Date:

How we spent our time together:

When I will come again:

Visitors

Who's visiting:

Today's Date:

How we spent our time together:

When I will come again:

Visitors

Who's visiting:

Today's Date:

How we spent our time together:

When I will come again:

Visitors

Who's visiting:

Today's Date:

How we spent our time together:

When I will come again:

Visitors

Who's visiting:

Today's Date:

How we spent our time together:

When I will come again:

Visitors

Who's visiting:

Today's Date:

How we spent our time together:

When I will come again:

Visitors

Who's visiting:

Today's Date:

How we spent our time together:

When I will come again:

Printed in the USA
CPSIA information can be obtained
at www.ICGtesting.com
LVHW070029291023
762448LV00015B/739

Visitors

Who's visiting:

Today's Date:

How we spent our time together:

When I will come again:

Visitors

Who's visiting:

Today's Date:

When I will come again:

How we spent our time together: